PAUL LARSENS

# RAPID SKILL ACQUISITION

### The Ultimate Guide On How to Acquire New Skills, Learn The Secrets and Effective Methods on How to Learn New Skills You Need For Success

**Descrierea CIP a Bibliotecii Naţionale a României**
**PAUL LARSENS**
    **RAPID SKILL ACQUISITION**. The Ultimate Guide On How to Acquire New Skills, Learn The Secrets and Effective Methods on How to Learn New Skills You Need For Success / Paul Larsens. – Bucharest: Editura My Ebook, 2020
    ISBN

# PAUL LARSENS

# RAPID SKILL ACQUISITION

## The Ultimate Guide On How to Acquire New Skills, Learn The Secrets and Effective Methods on How to Learn New Skills You Need For Success

My Ebook Publishing House
Bucharest, 2020

# TABLE OF CONTENTS

# INTRODUCTION

"You will never change your life until you change something you do daily", said by the popular televangelist Mike Murdock. Once you arrive at the torturous decision of changing your career, do not waste more time dwelling on the rationale behind this decision.

Get all your acts together and think of better ways of giving yourself a set of career skills that can gear you up for a new life and a new career.

Beefing up your career skills is rather an essential step of achieving true success. There are some secrets that will aid you in acquiring these skills. Learning these secrets can be very beneficial indeed.

Once you have learned all these secrets, you are on your way to enjoying a better career, a sense of stability and more money. All of the time, energy and efforts in strengthening your career skills will be well worth the investment.

By strengthening your career skills, you can become one of the potential candidates that employers are looking for. Thus, it is important to pay attention to these secrets.

One of the first steps of acquiring a new set of career skills is arranging funds that allow you to attend a university or school. This is a big step to moving forward for you to obtain a new set of skills.

Taking it a step further than college is also important. You may want to check out some extracurricular activities such as clubs or maybe even participate in a volunteer event. These are just a couple of examples that can be very beneficial.

Although obtaining new career skills means spending money and time, the outcome will be most beneficial. Keep in mind, it will be a difficult task and will require longer hours.

There is also a plethora of courses that can help in getting your foot in the door to your career. You can gain specialization and expertise in a specific activity or field. Some institutions also offer courses that are highly effective in establishing a career. They are reliable in arming yourself with a set of career skills. It is important to look into many schools and check to see what each offers.

Through constant training and practice, you will be on your way to embarking on a new career. Beefing up your skills is proven to provide long-term benefits and offer you a stable job.

Learning and development are also needed in meeting the challenging demands of a career. There are some skills that will also need improvement. By focusing on these skills, you can improve and become a better person.

Mentoring or taking online and offline courses are also essential parts of beefing up your skills. Below are some of the secrets to learn to aid in strengthening your career skills for your success.

# CHAPTER 1

## CAREER SKILL BASICS

All employers are searching for potential employees who already have their basic career skills that serve as their foundation skills.

Here are the basics pertaining to your career skill to ponder on:

- **Reading**: You can understand, interpret and locate written information like graphs, schedules and manuals.

- **Writing**: You can communicate ideas, information, thoughts and messages effectively in writing. You can further create documents like manuals, flow charts, graphs, reports, directions and letters.

- **Mathematics/Arithmetic Skills**: You can further perform computations and face practical problems by means of choosing from a wide array of mathematical techniques.

- **Listening**: You can attend to, interpret, respond and receive verbal cues and messages.

- **Speaking**: You can communicate and organize ideas orally.

- **Interpersonal and Team Skills**

An applicant must be competent with verbal communication. Answering questions in a good and positive manner is a good point. There is a need to be direct to the point and demonstrate good skills as part of customer service. There is no need to be outgoing. There is only a need to know how to better communicate with coworkers, team members, customers and the management.

# CHAPTER 2

## WHERE DO YOU NEED IMPROVEMENT?

### *Synopsis*

Most people are holding jobs with various employers. They are also moving to various employment sectors throughout their working life.

Thus, there is a need to be flexible enough with the working patterns. There is a need to be prepared with the changing sectors or jobs for better opportunities. You need to have improvement that serves you in the long run.

Employers are looking for skills that often go beyond experience and qualifications. While your experience and education may make you eligible enough to apply for a job, you still need to have mixed skills.

For most employers, getting the right people is important. It is all about identifying the people with the right qualities and skills to fulfill their role and contribute to the success of the organization. You may be one of those candidates who have the "hard skills" and qualifications in managing your job role. However, employers are less likely to hire you without your soft skills.

Where do you need improvement? Below are some of the skills that you may need to improve.

### Employability

Employability skills serve as the foundation of your career. Organizations are spending a lot of money and time to train their staff for various positions. During high employment, employers give favor for applicants who have well-rounded employability skills.

### Interpersonal

Take the time to know if you lack in interpersonal skills. These are important skills used in interacting with a lot of people. With good interpersonal skills, you can actively participate as a team member. You can satisfy the expectations of your clients and your customers. You can have time to negotiate and make good decisions. You can manage your time efficiently and work effectively with other employees.

You will still need to hone your interpersonal skills that allow you to build rapport with clients and colleagues. This leads to a less stressful and better working environment.

### Communication

Employers are searching for people who have the means to communicate well, both in written and verbal. If you are applying for a job or looking for a promotion with a current employer, you need to best demonstrate your communication skills. If you do not excel in communication, you need to improve your communication skills by practicing writing skills with a wide array of people. You may also want to practice maintaining good eye contact while speaking to people. You also need to write succinctly and clearly. You also need to demonstrate different vocabulary and tailor the language to the audience. These are essential skills that must be improved to have less chances of misunderstanding.

If you do not have the ability of speaking and writing with conciseness and clarity, then you need to strengthen it up for your career. Communication skills are important along with creativity.

**Critical Thinking**

The ability of solving problems and making decisions can be a big asset to an employer. This is a desirable skill that must be developed. In problem solving and decision making there is a need to gather reliable information.

The ability of effectively planning and organizing time gets the job done effectively. With critical thinking skills, employers save more money and time.

Creative thinkers are inventive and innovative. They are more likely to create new ways of making systems, adding value to the working environment and devising new ways of doing things.

**Personal**

Personal development is about acquiring the right attitude towards the organization that you work for. Employers even look for people who are interested to learn and develop.

If you are not open to changes and learning, then this is one of the areas that you need to develop personally. If you are resistant to changes in an organization, this will serve as a hindrance to your successful career. Most of the jobs involve change. Employers prefer people who are flexible, patient, and adaptable and respond to change.

## Numeracy

Numeracy skills are important, regardless if you are considering a job that works with numbers. If you are not confident and competent in working with numbers, then you need to improve it. Always remember that it can be to your best advantage in different employment settings. Being able to analyze and understand data in various formats is considered to be a crucial skill in most organizations.

# CHAPTER 3

# ASSESSMENT TESTS
# FOR YOUR GIVEN CAREER

Assessment tests help in determining the best career option for a person based on the personality, aptitude, interest, skills and other factors. These help one in choosing a job that interests and motivates him or her. The tests are also useful in suggesting career options. As a result, a person finds a job where he or she utilizes his or her skills.

In these tests, there are certain questions about the style of working, skill level in different subjects, attitude, interest of a person and interaction with others. With a set of responses, the basic personality of the person is understood along with a list of weaknesses and strengths. This is now matched with the database of career options.

This still depends on the responses that a career choice is given. It is crucial to be honest when answering all these questions. This is to get the best answer, lying will only cheat yourself.

Assessment tests are different depending on the institution, website or person that administrate it. Interest tests, personality tests, skill tests and intelligence tests are among the tests utilized in career assessment. Every test has its set of questions for the career choice of a person.

These assessment tests serve as a guideline for a person. However, they are not utilized as the right answer. They may not always be right, so people should still trust their instincts. These are tools that help people in choosing a job where they can excel and be passionate about their work.

Here are a few of the assessment tests available:

**Interest Test**

This is considered to be the strongest of all tests. This is also helpful in assessing the career that is best suited for a particular person. This best suggests the job that motivates and interests people to become successful in their career.

In this interest test, there will be questions about the set of choices in different fields. This further determines the interest level of a person accordingly. The orientation of the person toward different jobs is being determined. He or she is guided in deciding on the right career choice.

People can beef up their career skills and choose a job that best fits their interests by taking an interest test such as an interest assessment, self- assessment exercise, career pipeline or a career interest inventory test.

### Skills and Aptitude Test

Aptitude tests help to further determine the skill levels of a person. These also assess their weaknesses and strengths. These tests contain analytical ability, verbal reasoning, technical skills, visual skills, language skills, numeric reasoning, and speed tests.

A person could be suited for designing, architecture, finance, law or any other career and science. The inherent aptitude for a specific subject is being tested. This also highlights the person who is weak, average and strong. Thus, the person can further build on the strengths that beef up his or her career skills.

- Career Aptitude Test

- Mathematics Skill Assessment Test

- Skills Search

- Ability, Intelligence and Aptitude Tests

- Skills Center

**Personality Tests**

Personality tests are being used to check the personalities of applicants. This is also useful in beefing up the career skills of a person in the existing working environment.

The tests that are being taken into consideration are the reaction and the basic characteristics that depend on the personality of a person. One person may be introverted, outgoing, a thinker and leader as well as much more.

Through these tests, people can further identify their personality type. This can lead them in beefing up their career skills and their personality. Among the most common tests utilized are My Life Goals, MMDI Questionnaire, Personality Test and My Life Goals.

# CHAPTER 4

## **GET MENTORING**

While beefing up your career skills, mentoring is proven to be essential for your career success. There are several mentors to utilize that range from CEOs to CMOs to college professionals. These people are instrumental to your career growth and success. They offer their time, care and commitment to improving your skills.

Great mentors have the knowledge and experience to guide a protégé or mentee. Mentors are valuable because they guide you on your career path. Whether you are an experienced professional or recent college grad, mentors are a valuable asset in your career toolkit.

How will you get started on creating a relationship with your mentor? Below are among the simple approaches to strengthen your career skills:

**Determine the Mentorship Goals**

Before you seek out a mentor, write down all your expectations and the role that you like your mentor to play in your life. Do you like a mentor who can help you with installing networking attempts? Do you like a mentor who can assist you in learning more about a particular industry? Or, do you like someone that provides guidance on how to be a real and successful entrepreneur? Are there areas of experience or specific skills in your career that further need improvement?

It is crucial to determine your set of objectives and goals. This is for you and your mentor to achieve together.

**Recognize a Good Mentor**

While trying to discover a good mentor, make way to look for someone that can aid in your personal growth. In addition, look for someone who is truly brilliant and has found success in many areas.

The most obvious mentor candidates are current and former bosses, college professors with whom you can establish a good relationship. They are the leaders that can beef up your career skills in any field of work.

In the entire process, bear in mind that you are not limited to a single mentor. You can choose to have a mentor for each stage of your career. There are multiple mentors that specialize in different areas.

**Request for Mentorship**

It is easy to approach a mentor candidate when you have known the person and have built an existing relationship with him or her. You can easily ask this person for meetings, whether at a coffee shop or in the office environment.

Communicate all of your career goals and identify some of the areas that you want to improve on. Explain that you have a high regard for your mentor's specific leadership, experience and skills. You would like to take the opportunity of learning from her or him. There is nothing wrong with asking this person to become your mentor.

If you do not personally know a person, it is a bit difficult but is not impossible to approach them for mentorship. The leadership and intelligence of a mentor can provide you with good insights on beefing up your career skills. You must be ready and motivated as a student being mentored.

Here are the other ways of approaching a potential mentor that you do not know personally:

- Ask a mutual friend for you to be introduced to a mentor. Establish mutual connections over the internet through LinkedIn, or ask particular people in the network if they know potential mentors.

- Contact a mentor. One of the most direct ways of contacting a potential mentor is through email. If you cannot get an email address, you can try reaching out with social networks, like a Facebook message or Twitter. If you still do not hear back, you can still follow up. Be more persistent; however, do not be annoying.

- Explore the different ways to crossing paths with your mentor. If your mentor is an online influencer, a professional organization member or conference speaker, you have to attend online and live public events. You must not stalk this mentor, but instead, be proactive about the opportunities where you have the opportunity of meeting your mentor.

If you are well-acquainted with the potential mentor, the important element is to show admiration on the things that he or she does. You also need to show enthusiasm for growth.

### Be a Commendable Mentee

Business people are successful and busy. They consider their time to be valuable. Thus, when a person has agreed to mentor you, you need to realize this privilege and honor. Give respect to the time of the mentor by doing the following:

- Come prepared. Before you go out and meet with your mentor, be careful in planning the questions and topics that you want to address. This must be done for you to have a focused meeting.

- Ask for suggestions in moderation. Reaching out too much signals a needy, high-maintenance and overall work for your mentor. In general, reach out only for advice on career decisions-not little challenges

- Be a Good Listener. Mentors are dispensing advice. You may sometimes take the advice and you may not. In either way, you have to listen and consider the advice.

Then, you need to explain if you have to choose taking the alternative route.

- Share your Development. Your mentor is gratified in your progress as a protégé or mentee. Thus, you need to make sure that your mentor learns about your career wins. These wins are the indirect or direct result of advice from your mentor.

**Show Your Gratitude**

Due to the reason that your mentor is taking all his time out of his or her busy schedule, you have to show your appreciation. Thank your mentor frequently. Verbal thanks are enough, however, make an effort to send small gifts or cards.

Once your career has progressed and you have met a lot of people, you may even introduce your own mentor to other business contacts or other mentors. Business professionals are always finding value in meeting same- minded people like them.

Ultimately, you may even reach a point in your career that someone has a need of your mentorship. If you think that the person is a worthy mentee, agree to mentor her or him. Then, pass all of the lessons you learn from your mentor.

# CHAPTER 5

## ONLINE COURSES

Strengthening your skills is important because a lot of people are competing for a vacancy. There is also a need to stay competitive in terms of knowledge and skills in your career if you are aiming to outperform other candidates.

Online courses are available by means of distance learning programs or online education. They provide you a better option of beefing up your career skills and in-depth knowledge in your career field.

Online courses provide advantages of allowing students to learn at their most convenient time. More so, attending online courses reduces the stress of travelling back and forth.

Online courses allow you to plan your pace of study for as long as you have an established internet connection.

Here are a few of the tips to consider when finding online courses that beef up your career skills:

### 1.  Accreditation and Reputation of Online School

The reputation of an online school adds value to your certification. If you are aiming to earn certification from a study program, you need to sign up to an online course that is offered by an online school with a good reputation. It must also be accredited by the Department of Education.

### 2.  Request the Details of the Course Before Enrolling

The online course that is being offered by one school may be different from another school. There is a need to review further about the course details to benefit most from it. Most of the online schools offer the course details for free.

### 3.  Credit Transferability

You should check the credit transferability of your chosen online school. The tuition fee is counted for every credit hour basis.

## 4. Hands-on Training or Lab Work

Other online courses require you to attend a hands-on session or face- to-face classes. You better check out the location and schedule where you will need to attend the physical classes or training.

Online courses that cover different career-related subjects offer you a better option of beefing up your career skills. Thus, you can stay ahead of the competitive edge and continue to land jobs.

# CHAPTER 6

## OFFLINE COURSES

Enhance your career skills by earning certificates from offline courses. While taking offline courses, you will also need to devote your time to strengthening your career skills. You can enhance your career skills by obtaining a degree from a university or college.

### Getting Information for Offline Courses

Once you have decided to enroll in offline courses, there are comprehensive resources available at these universities and colleges. Educational institutions have a lot of programs that are specially developed and designed for adults of all ages. There are programs and scholarships that come along with these courses.

### Short-Term Training Courses

Universities and colleges are among the places to rely on strengthening your career skills. However, there are still short-term courses that can provide you with long-term benefits. They can offer you a stable career in the near future. These classes can make you fit in meeting the demands of your career.

On the other hand, the road to strengthening your career skills may require you to face financial roadblocks.

Follow these practices that can give your career a lift without burying in a debt on student loan.

### 1. Shop Around for A School

Selecting the right program is important if you do not want to bury yourself in a student loan debt. This is one of the errors that some people face in beefing up their career skills.

It is also best to further investigate about the programs at a local community college, private and public schools and four-year universities. You only need to narrow down your search.

You can also compare the design and costs of an offline course program with an online course program.

If you feel hesitant about obtaining a graduate degree, you can still get a certificate. You can jump into a subject that interests you the most without committing your time to a degree program.

## 2. Do not get stuck on a Sticker Price

Fees and tuitions are the launching point in tallying up a cost of the program. Always remember to provide a space in your budget for rent, transportation, supplies, books and the like.

In comparing various programs, the mandatory charges and courses must also be included. This is for you to get the true cost of the offline course.

## 3. Fill out the Student Aid's Free Application

Although you are quite hesitant to borrow, the federal loans for students can permit that you need to work fewer hours and focus more on your course work. This way, you can complete your offline courses a lot faster. There are more flexible opportunities and repayment options that you can enjoy the most of.

### 4. Transfer Credits

If you have already collected credits from former degree attempts, you can then ask if they can be transferred. Certificate holders like you must see to it if the credit hours you have earned throughout the certificate course are transferable to a degree.

# CHAPTER 7

## LIFE LESSONS

Choosing a successful career path is important to everyone. You may be one of those who have spent most of your time planning and pursuing a career. Thus, choosing the right career is crucial to your overall satisfaction and happiness.

In achieving success in your career, there is a need to pay attention to life lessons as well. These can guide you through strengthening the skills that you need as you advance to the next level of your career.

There is no need to underestimate the things that are possible for you. You are the master of your career. Thus, you need to take time to do some self- reflecting, renewing or reinventing your career skills for your ongoing fulfillment and success.

With life lessons, you can help yourself in strengthening your career skills. Here are some of the tips to consider for you to appreciate your life lessons:

## 1. Appreciate the Success Last Year

Showing gratitude is one of the things that you have to pay attention to. Take the time to jot down all things that make you feel proud in your career. Undoubtedly, you have accomplished all these things.

While you acknowledge and appreciated your successes, you can go as far as giving yourself a big hug. Take the time to list your career accomplishments. If there are still areas in your career that you need to strengthen on, then pay attention to it.

## 2. Learn From Your Life Lessons

The things that you learned from your disappointments and successes are the major life lessons that are worthy and truly meaningful. You need to ask yourself how you have achieved your accomplishments.

All of the thoughtful answers uncover the strengths, behaviors and abilities you consistently demonstrated while becoming a success.

You also need to ask yourself about the things that you learned from your failures and disappointments. The answers will serve as an reminders to you. Doing so provides great motivation and inspiration for you. They can be simple guidelines such as:

1.  Remembering Only What Matters
2.  Valuing Every Relationship
3.  Saying Yes to the Next Step
4.  Trusting the Process

As you can see, you are your own source of wisdom. Just imagine all of the results that you can achieve from taking the time to learn from all your disappointments and accomplishments. Jot down three statements of advice for future success in your career. Keep it memorable and short. Keep it a positive statement.

## 3. Shift to a Powerful Paradigm and Pursue your Passions

There is a need to live from the truth that is within you. The most important aspect of being successful is by getting in touch with the things that keep on holding you back. This is more likely your limiting beliefs.

One of the common negative and limiting beliefs of people is saying that they are not good enough. This only sabotages their own success and blocks their ability of living their passions and achieving their goals.

Recognize all these limiting beliefs and let them be replaced by a truthful statement. It is also essential to ask for help in order to break through these patterns. This may even require a divine intervention.

### 4. Live According to Key Roles and Values

Being clear on the things that get you out of bed in the morning is essential. What do you think are the personal standards or principles that you live by? Remember that values are the drivers of your goals. What are those values that are important to your life?

The key to living a balanced life is the ability of integrating the values in your life roles. You need to identify your key role that remains to be your focus.

### 5. Set Your High Career in Life and Follow your Success

Your life roles and values are considered to be your supportive framework. They help you in setting inspiring professional and personal goals. Set your career goals by identifying the results that you want to achieve this year. Take all the time you need to write your career goals; take consistent action and monitor your success.

The five transformational principles and life lessons can make you:

1. Proactive leader of your career
2. Become a Visible Leader
3. Get the Promotions That you Deserve
4. Enjoy a Fulfilling Career That you Love
5. Maintain a Balanced Life.

"Everything in life is a vehicle for your own transformation. Use it!". This is stated by Ram Dass, a renowned spiritual teacher and author.

# CHAPTER 8

## SELF-ESTEEM

### *Synopsis*

All people experience pride with themselves in reaching their personal or career goals. One of the reasons why people continue to pursue their dreams and take risks is because they have the ability of taking pleasures in their achievements.

The pleasure and pride that people experienced are combined as self- esteem. Thus, self-esteem is crucial for you to reach your successful career. Self-esteem is about having the satisfaction and confidence in your abilities and skills. This is achieved through a series of personal success. This also helps you in coping up with the difficult challenges in life. This also gives you the faith of overcoming them.

Self-esteem is important for you to have a successful career. You need it at any stage of your career - whether you are a new employee, dealing with deadlines and stress and working with other people. You need to get self- esteem in order to reach your goals.

Luckily, there are a few of the steps to consider to building and strengthening your self-worth.

1. Make a plan where you can get a daily exercise and eat nutritional foods and balanced diet. Maintain a respect and care for your body. Your mind gets a lot of these benefits because they promote good and healthy thoughts about your self-esteem.

2. Engage in meaningful and fun activities to you. Participate in a hobby that you most enjoy. Better yet, volunteer at a shelter if you like to be with furry creatures. It is through nurturing your interests that reminds you of the things that matter to you.

3. Reward Yourself for your Career Achievements. You can do this by celebrating with friends, offering yourself with praise and getting a massage. Each time that you

recognize your own success, you build a better support system and stronger trust for yourself.

4. Create your list of achievements and successes. You can refer to this list in times that you are in doubt of yourself. This is one of the best ways of staying in touch with your strength. You now have the ability of overcoming obstacles.

5. Forgive yourself for the things that do not turn out well. When you are critical of your own efforts, this only serves as a way of chipping your self-esteem. You have to release shame or guilt feelings by making a room for confidence and poise.

These steps are useful in building and strengthening your self-esteem. This takes dedication and practice. However, the results are still worth of your own efforts.

Remember that your self-esteem is the most important asset to reaching your success. Thus, you do not need to forget it and fix it.

You need your self-esteem as you strengthen up your career skills. Working on your self-esteem is one of the secrets of being successful!

... and your self-esteem ... when you go to bed.
Working on yourself is never a waste of time
of a complicated...

9 786069 836767

Printed by Libri Plureos GmbH in Hamburg, Germany